WHISPERS

OF HER

HEART

WHISPERS

OF HER

HEART

ALEXANDRA VILLANUEVA

Halo
PUBLISHING
INTERNATIONAL

Halo
PUBLISHING
INTERNATIONAL

Halo Publishing International
8000 W Interstate 10, #600
San Antonio, Texas 78230

First Edition, March 2023
ISBN: 978-1-63765-373-9
Library of Congress Control Number: 2023904340

The information contained within this book is strictly for informational purposes. Unless otherwise indicated, all the names, characters, businesses, places, events and incidents in this book are either the product of the author's imagination or used in a fictitious manner. Any resemblance to actual persons, living or dead, or actual events is purely coincidental.

Halo Publishing International is a self-publishing company that publishes adult fiction and non-fiction, children's literature, self-help, spiritual, and faith-based books. We continually strive to help authors reach their publishing goals and provide many different services that help them do so. We do not publish books that are deemed to be politically, religiously, or socially disrespectful, or books that are sexually provocative, including erotica. Halo reserves the right to refuse publication of any manuscript if it is deemed not to be in line with our principles. Do you have a book idea you would like us to consider publishing? Please visit www.halopublishing.com for more information.

This book is meant for those young adults who feel the raging storm inside and those hopeless and helpless romantics who might be in over their heads. Overall, just for everyone to know, you're not alone.

I saw you

I saw all your pain

I watched Him torment you in ways

Unimaginable to me

                lol

I knew nothing

And now you're on your own

You're broken and all I can do

Is apologize for only being able

To hold you

Off I went

To the great wide sea

I envisioned its power and beauty

And I remembered

The boy

A separate ocean

My heart had dived into

Coming back to you is nothing less than the rise out of the waves and the crisp air that fills my lungs.

I'd parallel park with you any day. Nothing sounds better than beinginatightspacewithyou.

It's the mundane things

A brush of your hair

The water on your cheeks after a shave

How you walk into a room.

I love you more in everyday life

Than I ever could in any love story.

Like most rebel-idolizing, in-a-constant-fugue-state-of-awareness teenagers who are thrust into adult life while still holding the title Child, I survive merely off energy drinks, the air of parental disappointment, and Skittles.

A jagged little thing of scarlet

Cold, thin, unforgiving steel

How strange the relief I feel

Just to see the pearls run down

And taste iron

Open your eyes

Yes, it's real

Yes, they exist

No, don't run and hide

Open your eyes

How ironic to be someone's happily ever after

When they're just your previous chapter

Reading others' words is one kind of peace. Creating my own is another entirely, and one I will revel in until the end of ever.

I promise to not let any harm come to you.

But how do I protect you from the monster inside your head?

Fireworks are nothing more than thousands of stars we have bottled up for our own amusement.

I was so busy trying to help build you up that I didn't notice you tearing me down.

You deserve nothing less, my darling

Past tense can refer to anyone—the dead or the gone. Sometimes they're one and the same.

I am made of you and him and her and all
the rest of them.

We were like seasons. A sweet spring that grew our roots, the hot, quick summer that fed our passion, the cool autumn that settled our life. But when winter came and you stole the warmth away, you turned me into a chilled, hollow little thing whose petals no longer had the strength to hold together.

Simple: The laughter wasn't worth the price of the pain.

Always in a daze

Through the days

No telling how much it all weighs

Or in how many ways

I look for a hopeful raise

Instead of a dreadful raze

Like the seasons, we changed

The dead parts of us falling away with

The autumn leaves

Making room for us to hibernate

In each other's hearts

I always said we were like family—I just never realized it was the kind of family that left people behind.

Him: You know I would give you the world.

Her: But it's not yours to give.

It was easier to say he never tried

Than it was to believe he had tried for the both of them

Out of everything of mine you broke, my heart was the easiest to heal.

Hope is my friend, Love is my companion

As sure as the Sun is high in the Sky

Touch never meant anything to me until
I realized yours was the only kind I ever
wanted to grace my skin.

The tears that never fell burned my throat more than any whiskey.

You are all my favorite characters, simply sprung from the page and given a heartbeat.

Life is more than one person……isn't it?

Maybe the Queen of Hearts didn't want the roses to just be red. Maybe she wanted to see them bleed.

Though my heart breaks leaving you, it heals the moment I hold you again.

Lavender should help anxiety/Because of you/It grows mine as much as/The garden it lives in

Growing up I was bound by the law. Today
I bind it to you.

Hey, can you pull over? The world has grown some art, and you should take a piece home with you.

Lady Justice may be blind, but I still put my faith in the deadly point of her sword.

Books are my sustenance; the ink on the page is no more than the bread for my body.

They say picking up someone else's pieces will just get you cut. They don't understand that it can be easier than gluing yourself back together.

You're looking from

The outside

In

You see the walls

Still standing

Up

Your view is better

All I see

Is the glue on each

Crack

Atlas, my dear Titan, I simply break when
I feel the world on my shoulders...

If she never gave birth, is she still a mother?

If she chose to give it up rather than be chosen by a higher power and have it taken from her, is she still a mother?

Did the milk that still fell from her breast belong to a child that never lived outside her womb?

If she denied the beating drum that matched her own, is she still a mother?

If her body healed but her mind shattered, does she still hold the title Maternal?

Is she still Mother if her child never became?

It's the days I sit

And breathe

In

Out

In

Out

And soak in

The rays of optimism

That shine down on me

Uniform Independence

We are all the same; we are all different

I wonder

If you put a skull

Up to your ear

Would you hear

The ocean

Or the empty

Floating

Thoughts

Of the person

Left behind

Hope is an infectious disease that targets your most sensual dreams and inhibits your common sense.

The dark and shadowed voice of my conscience is silenced by your slow, simple bated breath.

What is love?

It's how they move

How they feel

How they listen

How they dream.

It's the way they speak

The way they hope.

It's the very air they breathe.

You wrote your love across my skin in the invisible ink of your fingertips.

Sometimes they give you nightmares. They make you cry and scream and itch at your skin. But sometimes they give you dreams that are brought to life by the smallest things.

Thursday flowers meant everything to me.
But then they took everything from me.

I found a pink one. And you made me love it. But I'm taking it back. I discovered a piece of myself back then. I am simply rediscovering it without you.

I love how you Believe. I love how you follow Him. And how you accept me and that I don't. I love your trust in Him, and I'll stand by you as your witness, and you may lead me, though I know you understand that I may not be behind you.

Mommy, what's God?

Sweetheart, God is whatever you believe Him to be. God is your daddy, but not your mommy. You can be Him, but you don't have to be. All that matters is know you are loved. By me, by your daddy, and if you choose, by Him.

I could feel the relay running circles

Always ahead or behind but we never quite

Met

And I longed for a second to see your eyes

It would have felt like breath in my lungs was

Pure

And the beating of my heart would have

Doubled

But I would have known we would be okay

If I had been able to catch you

And look at you

Getting shot in the arm leaves a bruise.
It's nothing like your kisses though. How
I wish for those to scar.

The Fates may have written your story, but you weave your own path of destruction.

The chaos in your soul lights the fire behind your eyes.

Sometimes I can feel them on my back

Longing to open

And feel the air

And I think that if I close my eyes

One day I'll just go

Up, up, up

To the cloud and the sky

And never come down

Every cent

Every dollar

Every gift

Everything I can

It's all yours.

Shower.

Bury.

Spoil.

Rotten.

In my mind

On my skin

In my room

On my heart

You've given me

Yourself

So I'll paint you

As the angel

You are

It felt like the old ways did—nostalgia and peace and a forever-lingering sense of pain.

She cried in pain as she said goodbye, knowing his name would forever be etched into her heart.

The Sky said goodbye to the Earth, and it was us who caught her tears.

She sat in the Garden of Darkness and watched as the flowers shone down on her.

You're the stars I've tried so hard to reach.

When you looked at me, I knew you had stripped me of every guard I put up. You saw my soul in the blink of an eye.

You're poison to my mind and a balm for my heart.

There are demons behind the eyes of those who smile to wash away another's tears.

I carry my heart around like a bag full of the stars… If I let it go, they're going to spill all over the cosmos.

He spoke with the same language, but the melody of his words still drove me mad.

He embodied my childhood heroes, and
I yearned to love him more than by the
ink he was written in.

If you walk away, you will walk the line of my heartbeat.

Say what you will. A young heart in love is still a heart in love.

365 days and I'm still living through the moment we met.

I thought you were good. But even angels will act like devils to get what they want.

We aren't princesses and princes in this world. But to each other I know we mean more than any kingdom there is.

All my love for you lies in the brokenhearted melodies of a Luke Bryan song.

We are two souls that will never be close enough.

Perhaps the reason I can't stand the silence on my own is because it's so loud when I'm not.

I need you to squeeze all my hurt pieces together and never let me go.

Distance can kill a person. And you're not even gone yet.

We might have been running away, but in the end, just trying to get home.

There is no rehab to escape a drug that has a beating heart.

All the books in the world would never fill my heart as much as you do.

The cortisol in my veins

Stings like volts in a wire

And only released

By the metal of a paper-thin

Conductor

Stripping the cord

I don't measure my calendar in days and events, but in minutes spent with you.

I may not know exactly what my worth is,
but I definitely know what it isn't.

I am a strong person who is looking for
someone she can be happy with, not
just someone who will screw around or
choose her just because she's the best
option at the moment.

You say you want me; then show me.
Show me by treating me as if I'm a
person you want and deserve to have.

*Chase me like nothing else in
your life except your dreams.*

Buy me flowers, or, hell,
pick some from the side of the road.

Write me little notes to find that
make me smile throughout the day.

Plan a night out and
take me to dinner.

You don't need to spend money to
show that you care. You need to
spend some effort.

Put thought into it. Get a piece of paper and use your brain, Scarecrow.

Plan a picnic.

Build me a fort.

Write me a letter.

Treat me how you want a girl to treat you. I would give all of my energy, but I won't keep it up if I don't get some of that same energy in return.

Romance me, make me swoon, dance with me in the middle of the street. Even if you can't dance. Kiss me for no reason. Hold me as if you could never let me go.

Love me. Love me in my simplest form.

I know I'm not easy, but no one ever is. I would try my hardest to give you the world if you asked for it. All I'm asking is for you to try. Then try harder.

And when you think there's nothing else you could do, think some more.

Because there always is.

The smallest of things could change everything. The bar is on the floor, and it shouldn't be.

The bare minimum should not be acknowledging that I exist.

Chase me, make me love you, make me never be able to imagine a world without you. I'm ready for it.

Are you?

One sharp breath. Four words, 17 letters…
How easily you could overdose. You are
my addiction

I should have read it to you. I should have given you that piece of me. More and more, you are my personal "host of golden daffodils." (William Wordsworth)

"Your dad still sees you as a kid?" My darling, I'll be playing dress-up with him until the day he goes.

Blowing in the wind

Up, up, up

It's flying to you, my love

I'll send my words to the stars

Just so you know I'll never forget

You're my angel up in the sky

You talk about me in a way that doesn't matter

But you touch me

With such care and grace

All your attention pours from those fingertips

Thousands of times more than

From your lips

I get so lost in it

That I forget about

The silence

I've made a list

Just little details

13 short lines

Trivial things

But, darling,

They are what make you

The man I want to

Love

My darling little girl

Look how far you've come

We still struggle

But wait until

You see what's in store

Neither the Sun or Moon

Could match the shine

You'll show this world

You say three months

I say two

You say purple

I say blue

We're just starting

And we don't even have a clue

It's a shallow voice in the back of my mind

Sometimes only about a whisper

Otherwise, a constant siren

I tell myself the opposite of its words

But I grow weary of the repetition

Can I please just have

A break?

I've been chipped

S h a t t e r e d

And broken

The glue in the old holes

Always looked ugly

But now

I make them

B e a u t i f u l

Filling my broken parts

With the sun's golden rays

What I once saw as trash

Now a rueful piece of kintsugi

I was blindly in love once

A hopeless heart that was in your hands

But then you took it with you

And I'm empty now

Please give it back

It was yours to keep

Until I found my sight

To set it

To see it spread

Darling the only inferno I want raging

Is the one you have burning for me

Long distance isn't dating miles apart

It's just dating my cell phone

Honey you can either fail or succeed, but you gotta give yourself the chance to do one.

Just thinking about dancing with you

Feeling your body against mine

Seeing the river in your eyes

You're the mate to my mind, body, and soul

1,2,3,4

I declare a love war

You say you love me more

But you make me burn

In my very core

It's time

To share with you

My deepest secrets

The valleys of my being

And I don't know

If you'll try to climb up them

Or trek right through

These vicious hells

Muse

A simple word

For which I lack any definition

Besides this world

Around me

To yield

Is to drop my sword

Alas

I've fought too hard

To kneel at the feet of surrender

It's a dark garden

That grows briar and ivy

Hurting you and trapping you

But one day

Maybe you can calm it

Enough to grow

Some

Dandelions

You love to come

When it's cold and dark

But I know your weakness

It is the hearth

That shines upon me

And the strength

It gives me

Congrats!

You've raised the bar

But, hey,

Could you please not play Double Dutch?

Just because something is beautiful doesn't mean it won't steal your soul while you look at it.

Save your lies for the Devil. He's fluent.

There you are, right in front of me

Yet my outstretched arms

Blindly looking to grab hold

Everywhere

But forward

Follow your demons

To the heavens they were sowed, not the hell from which they were reaped.

You might climb Mount Everest.

You might climb the stairs.

You might just climb out of bed.

But you did it.

I'm proud of you.

Use your brain, little Scarecrow,

You've got at the courage you need at heart.

The Big Dipper has 8

Ursa Major has 18

You, my darling,

Are covered in stars

And I will make

Thousands of constellations

Just for you

The amount of hate I have for you

I will equal that

And more

In the love I have for myself.

The pain you caused me

Will be the ground

From which I'll grow.

Home is where the heart is

But I need a map and a compass

Because I'm lost